RELL JERV
Mission Incomplete

Cassandra JerVey

authorHOUSE®

AuthorHouse™
1663 Liberty Drive
Bloomington, IN 47403
www.authorhouse.com
Phone: 1 (800) 839-8640

Published by AuthorHouse 06/08/2018

ISBN: 978-1-5462-4526-1 (sc)
ISBN: 978-1-5462-4525-4 (e)

I dedicate this book to Rell Jerv, his creative production team, Masina Music Makers (TheMak3rs), and anyone else who has overcome obstacles and has proven themselves to be unstoppable.

MY STORY

Some people are fortunate enough to have all that they desire and need. I, on the other hand, had to work for it. Through blood, sweat, and tears I had to earn it. "What don't kill you makes you stronger." At least that's what I was told. If that's the truth, I have the strength of Goliath, the mighty giant. I have the strength of the Incredible Hulk. I guess that would explain why the things that I've been through only made me crack but never made me crumble. My struggles in life have definitely made me a stronger man, a better man. I had to live by certain fundamentals to get by. I learned how to cope and to make due with whatever came my way. No use in making excuses in life. Who would even listen? It was the hand that I was dealt, and I had to play it. There were certain things that was destined to happen in order for me to become who I am today. But, at the end of the day, I never let my situations predetermine my future. I would have been a fool if I would have let that happen. I always knew that there was something that existed far beyond what the eye could see. The battle wasn't what I could or couldn't see, the battle was staying focused.

My name is Derrell, but most people know me by Rell, and my stage name is Rell Jerv. What is it that I do? I'm glad you asked. I rap. Not just any kind of rap but I rap with meaning. I tell a story. My story...my way. A story that only can be told by me. A story that only could be seen through the deep corneas of my eyes. Everybody won't be willing to take this ride with me because they don't understand. That doesn't surprise me because everybody wasn't meant to understand. However, I'm sure that a lot of people can relate to my life. I'm sure that many people can relate to the everyday struggle of trying to make a dollar out of $0.15 and make it stretch to the next week. It takes a strong minded person to keep a dream alive and try to become something great while facing poverty.

I didn't really have nothing growing up, but I always knew I was going to be something. Just because I wasn't born with a silver spoon in my mouth didn't mean I had to be a product of my environment. That's where a lot of people seem to go wrong. Just because you come from a rocky place doesn't mean that your life has to be rocky. You can look at things and use it as an example of what not to do. Whenever I see people make bad decisions that can cause themselves to be incarcerated or decisions that can be hurtful to someone else, I use that as an example to not go down that path. I'm heavily influenced to do the polar opposite and make the right decisions that would bring me closer to accomplishing my goals. It's a mind thing. You have to be able to control your mind and tame your thoughts. I don't have time to figure out how to make my dreams come true from behind bars. I'm not built for prison and I never intend on going.

I've always tried to live my life according to how I felt life should be lived. People judge me. So. They don't always agree with the way I live my life and how I make moves. But hey, it's my life. I'm living my life with no regrets. I don't live my life to satisfy people. If your focus is to satisfy people you will be living a miserable life. People will be with you one minute and gone the next. They will judge you if you're doing good or if you're doing bad. You just can't win. That's why individuals should do what they want to do and never let people hinder their dreams.

My Dreams

I have dreams, big dreams, and everything that I have been through in my life has conditioned me to chase this dream. My dream, like many others, is to be one of the greatest rap stars out here. What sets me apart from the others is my dedication. I dedicate every fiber of my being to my craft. I stay up late and wake up early to perfect my craft. I would have multiple streams of employment so that I could fund my music and make ends meet at the same time. You can always tell how bad somebody wants something by the way they go after it.

Writing lyrics is so naturally easy for me. I can hear a beat and the lyrics just automatically come. I can hear a beat that reminds me of a time in my life and the rhymes just start to flow. That's a creative ability that some people don't have. I thank God for all of my gifts and talents that he has blessed me with. I would consider it robbery to myself if I didn't utilize the creativity that I was born with. I tried to live an average life by working and going to school like everybody else, but it just wasn't what I wanted. That lifestyle wasn't working for me. Unfortunately, I couldn't give up on that 9-5 lifestyle because I had responsibilities. When something eats at you long enough, after a while, you'll make some changes. I feel like I was put here to make a difference through my music, and that's what I will do until that dream is accomplished.

Taking a Chance

Life is about choices. Some choices will be good ones and some will be bad ones. The thing about choices is that you might not know what the outcome will be. That's when you have to take a chance and jump. When you take that chance, and the outcome is not what you want it to be, you just dust yourself off and try again. You keep on trying until the outcome is favorable. But, most importantly, you can't be afraid to try. People don't succeed because they give up before they even try. The task at hand looks too big so it becomes intimidating. You can't be afraid to take a chance. Making mistakes is how people learn in life. If a person hasn't made mistakes they are not learning. The learning aspect of it all might not happen right away, but one day, the light bulb will come on.

Taking chances can be hard and making changes can be difficult. Change can be a scary thing because it takes us away from what we're used to and pulls us out of our comfort zone. Being afraid to take a chance can paralyze a person from fulfilling their goals in life. That's one thing I never had to deal with because I was never afraid. My issue was having patience for the bigger picture at the end of the tunnel to get a little closer where it was more tangible. I wanted to quit because things weren't taking off for me like I thought they would. Therefore, the process was hard and sometimes disappointing. But, once again, the dedication is what sets me apart from many artists. Even when nothing was happening I still kept at it.

There was a point in my life where I was chasing a dream, but I didn't know what I was chasing. I always say that people live so much of their lives with their head down. For a long period of time, I didn't even remember a lot of my work. It seemed like I blinked and I was here. I would have to really sit and think to remember, or I would have a dream or a conversation that would remind me of something that I did. For a long time, I was numb. That's why it's so important to me to feel everything throughout this process of reaching my dreams. I'm trying to feel every moment, every accomplishment, and every situation whether it's good or bad. In the last year or so, I have been very emotional because I'm trying to feel everything. I was numb because of everything that I went through and saw in my life. So now, I am learning how to live in the moment and just take everything in.

"WHAT DON'T KILL YOU MAKES YOU STRONGER"

I can honestly say that I know who the people are that truly believes in me and stands behind me. I'm grateful to have the love and support of my mom. My mom....she is my best friend. We have always been close. It's always been me and her. My mom and I went through some difficult things in the past. Like all kids and their parents they have their differences at some point. I left the house for a while and slept on somebody's floor. But, I always ended up coming back. That's my mom...and the ultimate goal for any real man is to provide for his family and give back to his mother. If nobody else, I want to buy my mom a house, take her on vacation, make sure she has money in her bank account, and make sure she has nice things.

It was hard growing up with a single mom. I didn't have all the things that a lot of people had and I didn't go all the places other people went. My mom worked a lot. As much as she worked there was no way to keep tabs on us. It was hard not being able to see my mom during the day before I went to school. When I got home from school I would pick up my younger sister from the bus stop and bring her home, feed her, bathe her, and wait up for my mom to get home at midnight. I hardly ever saw her. Even though, my mom worked a lot, we had really bad financial problems. It wasn't easy coming home to a dark house because there was no electricity or a house that had no food. The struggle was real. I remember one time in particular when I went to breakfast before school. Afterwards, when I got off the bus to come home, my mom, her boyfriend, and my uncle picked me up in a truck from the bus stop. When we pulled up to the house it was all boarded up. I didn't understand what was going on. I just sat there trying to figure out what was happening.

"Why is the house even boarded up?" I asked out loud. Nobody answered.

Then, my mom, her boyfriend, and my uncle unscrewed the boards so they could get all of our stuff out. I didn't understand because everything was fine when I left that morning. I was confused. After they got all of the stuff out we moved it to my nana's house. This is why I go so hard at chasing my dream. My experiences have lit a fire under me to constantly go hard and never give up. I don't ever want to end up back there. I don't ever want to be put in a position of vulnerability where somebody can take everything away from me. It was hard having to stay with people and not have our own space. I know that I can't predict the future, but I'm trying my best to make my future better than my past. We jumped from having our own house to staying at my Nana's house, and going from place to place. All that back and forth and not really being stable having our own place...

I met some kids when I was staying at my aunt's house in New Jersey. Their biggest worry for some of them was that their mom didn't buy them new sneakers or that there wasn't enough Gatorade in the house. I thought to myself, *you just don't understand how good you got it.* Unless you've experienced some of these things you couldn't begin to understand what it's like for a kid to have to figure out what tomorrow may bring.

My mom never knew how much the instability and her always working and not being there bothered me. We never had "that talk." Now, as an adult, I understand the sacrifice. I watched her struggle each and every day. And yet, in the midst of all the struggles, I still had my hopes and dreams. Despite everything we went through God still came and made something beautiful out of my life.

My mom did her best to take care of me and my siblings since I had a failed relationship with my dad. He always dropped me off at Shirley's house. We had a weird relationship. I felt like whenever I was over her house she would feed me and let me watch television just because she felt like she had to do it because I was there. I never remembered her doing anything with me. One day when I was left there, I got so mad that I punched through a thick glass and cut my hand and wrist all up. My Uncle Aaron cleaned up my hand and bandaged it up. I don't even remember how I made it home that day. All I know is I got there somehow without anybody's help. Every time I was dropped off I was always with my Uncle E or Uncle Aaron, which is why I was close to them. Uncle Aaron would sit and watch football and the Sixers games with me and teach me about sports. When my uncle Aaron passed away it really hurt me because he was like a dad to me.

When I was about 9 or 10 years old we were all piled in the car to go to the movies one afternoon. Before we left my phone rang. It was my dad.

"Hello?" I said.

"Yo, son. I'm about to come and get you so we can go out. Make sure you're ready I'm on my way," he said to me.

"Alright cool." I hung up the phone and turned to my mom.

"Mom, I'm going to stay here because my dad just called and said he's about to come and get me."

"Are you sure...because we're still gonna go? But, if you wanna wait here you can wait here."

"Yeah, he said he's on his way." I got out the car and sat on the step.

I sat on the front step outside and watched the car pull off. I sat there motionless and waited. I literally waited outside until it got dark and he never showed up. My mom came back from being out and she saw me still waiting outside.

"What happened?" she asked curiously.

"He never came." She sucked her teeth and walked in the house.

I didn't even cry. From that moment...I was done. For a long time, I carried that pain. I never understood how people can say they've been through pain and all they know is pain. It never made sense to me that a person could go through pain and turn around and inflict the same kind of pain on a person. Especially, somebody that's a part of me...someone that came from me. That doesn't make sense to me. Feeling that pain...I know how it feels because I went through it, and I don't want my kids to feel that kind of pain. To be the best father that I could possibly be is always in the back of my mind.

THE BLOODLINE

I've been grinding for about 10 years and there are a selected few who has always believed in me and supported me. They know who they are. Since, all of the attention, I have newly found friends and family members that have crawled out of their cracks and crevices to claim relationships with me. People are claiming to be close to me just because they share the same last name as me or because they simply know of me. If you haven't called to see if I'm alive or if you haven't called to check on me in months, then you're not worthy of being family. I don't know you. How old am I? Do you know when my birthday is? Someone even asked me how we were related? There have been family members that saw me on television, and I clearly said how old I was, and they're still asking me how old I am. There was another family member that put me on spotlight at a funeral trying to give me props. *Really? At a funeral? Who does that?* I thought. He must have forgotten the last time I saw him I was cussing him out at the big blow up at my granny's repass. There was never no apology, no conversation or nothing. Now all of a sudden, I'm the best thing since sliced bread. For people that are just trying to show up, I just separate myself...I'm so in my own bubble and I don't have a problem with saying no to people.

My siblings and I are very close. I am the fourth child out of six other siblings. It was hard being the middle child because I felt like I always had to be perfect. My mom would always call me a little genius. Truth was, I didn't want to be a genius I just wanted to be normal. That kind of pressure was crazy. It was too much for a child to handle. I felt like the expectations were too high for a child. But, as I look at my life now, I guess by being called a genius prepared me to walk in greatness.

Even though, my siblings and I didn't all live together growing up, we communicate quite often. We've always had a relationship. That's more than what I can say about my half-siblings, considering I don't even know who they are. Even being through fights and stuff like that we've never been mad at each other long enough not to talk. Despite of everything we've been through personally and as children we still maintain an unconditional bond that cannot be broken.

Fatherhood

When I was younger, I always said if I ever had kids I would never want them to go through what I went through. Before I'm anything to anybody else I'm a father to my kids, first. I have two kids who I really love. They mean the world to me. I grind every day for them so they won't have the same struggles I did. I had my daughter when I was 17 years old. I graduated from high school 3 weeks before she was born. I was making only $200 a week. I didn't know what I was going to do...and just kind of figured it out. Three years later, I was blessed with a son. I love being able to watch them be happy as they grow up. I go to different functions that are going on at my daughter's school, and I'm happy to do that. It's important to me to be an involved parent because I didn't have that.

Around the time my daughter was born I was mentally in a bad place. There was a point in time when I didn't care about nothing. I didn't care about life. I had no emotions. If you were to look me in my face you would see no emotions...nothing. I was just going through life. When my daughter came and fatherhood hit me I really had to buckle down. I realized that the streets were not the place for me.

My greatest accomplishment is the father that I am to my kids. Being able to see my kids every day, driving them to school, and making sure they grow up happy is an accomplishment by itself. It is my biggest goal to make sure they don't ever have to live through what I had to live through and experience anything that I had to experience when I was younger. It doesn't take much to make a child happy. They know that they are loved and well taken care of. They also know that I do what I do to make sure they have a comfortable life and a bright future.

Relationships

Unfortunately, things didn't work out between my daughter's mother and me. I fought for 5 long years trying to get custody of her. After a long hard battle, I finally was awarded custody. After a short engagement to my son's mother that relationship didn't work out either.

At this point in my life, it's hard for me to be in a relationship with anyone. My main focus is to get where I want to be with my music and to be able to provide for my family. Throughout my career, it was hard to invest in a relationship with people who didn't understand the time it takes to develop a craft like this. It takes a special person to understand that the type of drive and ambition that I have doesn't always allow time to be build a relationship.

Sometimes it takes putting in 12-hour days or more in the studio. The amount of time that I spend in the studio varies if I'm working on a project. If I'm not working on a project I will spend about two days a week in the studio for a few hours just to play around with some records. When I am focused, I get locked in and deflect everything. I understand that it's hard for them to allow me to do what I do, but a dream like this takes work and dedication. It takes a strong person to be able to accept my work ethic and everything that comes with the territory. It's important to have the right person to fit into the puzzle of my life. That missing piece has got to be 100% compatible to who I am and understand my needs. Being compatible is important. I need someone that has that fire, that drive, that desire to work hard and to want more out of life. I can't be satisfied with somebody that doesn't have any ambitions or somebody that's comfortable with being a bump on a log. At this point in the game, it's hard to find that genuine person. So, for now, I am just focusing on my work and if something that once was gets rekindled in the process or if something else comes along... it comes along. But it's not my focus right now. I feel like it could be another distraction. I must put all my energy into the window of opportunities that are being opened before me. There are a lot of things that I'm learning to do in this process, and I don't have enough space on the plate to add a relationship.

FULFILLING THE VOID

It's hard for a boy to grow up to be a strong man without another strong man to help guide them. Thankfully, I had male role models and other people throughout my life that I could turn to at different points in my life. They tried their best to keep me on the right path and teach me how to reach my goals.

There was a special someone by the name of Bob that God put in my life to help guide me. I called him my grandpop because he filled a void in my life in many ways. He was somebody I really looked up to. I could talk to him about anything. He was there for my family for a long time in more ways than people even know. We were able to lean and depend on Bob for anything. When he came into my life he took me under his wing and would tell me how smart I was and that I could do anything I wanted to do.

"You can speak, you're smart, you know what you want to do you just have to stay focused," he said.

Bob had his own cleaning and moving company, which was very successful. He came from nothing, started his own business, and did very well for himself. I first met him when my mom started working with him. He would always ask me to help him out on his moving jobs. We used to have so many personal conversations when I was out with him. We had conversations about my goals and he would tell me about the things he went through in his life. He was able to relate to me because we went through similar things. I loved having somebody that could relate to me rather than just talk. Bob believed in me. It meant a lot to have somebody else besides family believe in me. This was somebody I respected and looked up to. A lot of family members said that they believed in me, but that's what they're supposed to do. Those are the things that they are supposed to say. Bob was such a kind hearted person to everyone. He would help people move and wouldn't charge them anything. He understood the struggle and knew that the struggle was real to a lot of the clients that he dealt with. I tried to stay busy working as much as I could in order to stay out of the streets. Even when I wasn't helping him on his jobs he would still come and pick me up. I was getting into a lot of fights in the streets and I saw where my life was headed if I didn't make some changes. It was important that I stayed out of the streets because I didn't care about nothing and I didn't fear nothing, and that was a very bad way to be.

One day, my mom told me to come over to help out because Bob was going to bring some furniture over in the morning. So, I went over there early in the morning before I went to work. I waited as long as I could but I needed to leave.

"Mom, I waited as long as I could but I got to get to work."

"Alright," she said.

It's not like him to just not show up. He always kept his word, I thought. "Maybe something came up. Maybe he had another job or something. But, I need to go or I'm going to be late for work," I said.

As soon as I got to work and clocked in my mom called me. "Rell, Bob passed away."

I just dropped right onto the floor. Basically, he got up that morning, started the truck and went back in the house to sit down while the truck warmed up. His wife made him a cup of coffee and they were sitting down talking. Minutes later, he went silent and passed away sitting in his chair...about to come. I was so excited and looking forward to seeing him because I hadn't seen him in months because I was doing my own thing and working. I've been meaning to catch up...but then, boom. Whatever I was going through I could always talk to him. It's hard when you have that crutch that you've leaned on for so long pulled out from underneath you and you're left standing on your own.

There was another family friend who I started to get really close to. He called himself Cool Jerk because that's what he was. His real name was Larue. I don't even know when our relationship started he just sort of took me under his wing like Bob did. I would go to his house after school and watch television. I would make some Oodles of Noodles and we would sit on the couch and just talk for hours. Larue was a father figure to a lot of people in my family. He was always the type of person that had jokes about everything. People always wanted to be around him because he was a cool person and he would always say the craziest things. I remember one night when I was sleeping on his couch and *That's So Raven* came on. That was the first time I had ever seen that show. He told me like it was...he was real, he didn't hold nothing back from me. So, for a period of time, I wanted to be with Larue. Shirley was in the same complex with him and I didn't even have a relationship with her. I didn't even go to her apartment to visit her. What for... to be nonexistent? When Larue suddenly passed away I was hurt all over again. It just brought back the pain that I was still feeling about Bob passing away.

First, I was with my Uncle Maine, but he was dealing with whatever he was going through and couldn't be there for me. I needed somewhere else to go. That's when I started to get close to my Aunt Quetta. Then, she ended up moving to Pittsburgh to go to school to pursue her culinary degree. Later on, my younger sister's dad, Duane, who also played an important role in my life, moved to New York. All over again, I was by myself. I felt lost and hopeless. I felt like everybody I got close to ended up leaving. It's hard being in a world when you feel like you don't have anybody to lean on or anybody to talk to.

THE STREETS

I never sold drugs or nothing like that. I was just running around in the wrong circle. I was hanging with people that I had no business hanging around with and getting into trouble. I think at some point in every young man's life they become curious about the streets and start to get involved. I could never get too deep into the streets because I always had a conscious, which most people in the streets don't have. I was a thinker. I would be about to get into something that I knew I had no business getting into and I would begin to think about the consequences. Some people act, and then, think. But, I think before I act.

There are times when I get road rage and I want to jump out my car to yell at the other driver, but my conscious takes control of me. Thankfully, it does because that's a situation that could definitely end terribly wrong.

I remember when I was younger me and a few guys planned to break into a shoe store. It all sounded well and good when we talked about it, but once again, my conscious took control when the time came to actually do it. The first thing I thought was, *Man, there are cameras in here.* So, I never went in.

I never saw myself as a criminal or just another "street kid." It was just one of those things where I wanted to see what it was like to get a taste of the streets. When it came to stuff like fighting I wasn't scared of nobody. But, when it came to stuff that could alter my life or ultimately put me in jail, I was very conscious about it. I was always conscious about getting locked up. Even when I didn't do anything wrong or simply walk pass a cop I am still conscious of my every move. Maybe it was because other people I knew was always in and out of jail so many times…I don't know. The first time I went to visit someone in prison was a horrible experience. It was something about the whole process that did something to me. Having to go through the process of being searched, seeing the barbed wire, hearing the buzzing of the gates…it was way too much, so I know for sure that prison is one place I never want to go. There's way too much in this world that I want to do and explore, and I cannot be stuck behind four walls.

The assumption is that life is easier in the streets, but it's really not. Living a hard knock life is more dangerous than any other legit job in the world. The streets don't care about anybody and a bullet doesn't have anybody's name on it. You have to be careful where you go and who you deal with. Everybody doesn't have your best interest at heart and you never know when trouble is going to come. Sometimes you may get away with your life, sometimes you won't. Fortunately, for me, I did.

One time, an incident happened when me and one of my brothers could have lost our lives. We'd just left our uncle's house and was walking down the street when we walked passed a group of guys that was standing on the corner. My brother recognized one of the guys because they had bad history together. We were literally one block away from my uncle's house when my brother looked back and noticed that they started following us.

"Yo, that's Eric," Nell says to me. *Looks back.* "They're following us." *I look back.* "You ready?" he says letting me know that things were about to go down.

"It's whatever," I say reassuring him that I am ready to go to battle.

We walked down one more block, which was a dark block, and they started speeding up.

"Yo, you wanna run?" he asks me as he starts jogging.

I just stopped in my tracks and turned around. I don't even know why I stopped, but I turned and leaned on the hood of a car and just looked at them. They came riding up fast on their bikes, and then dropped them as they ran up to us pulling out their guns. They had two guns pointed at me.

"Yeah, what's up fool, what's up?" they yelled.

I didn't say anything. For some reason, I wasn't scared. I just looked them in their faces. One of the guys tried to go in my pocket to take my money and I slapped his hand away. I know that when someone is trying to jack you you're supposed to just give up whatever you have, but my first instinct was to slap his hand away. Then, it became one big brawl with all of us.

"Nell, Nell!" I yelled. He ran over and they scattered a little bit but everybody is still fighting.

When I looked up again I saw my brother on the ground. One of the boys picked up a recycle bin and was about to hit him with it. I ran over and hit the boy and picked Nell up off the ground and we ran. A few months later, one of the guys we were fighting was sentenced for a murder charge on another crime that he'd committed somewhere else. It was only the grace of God that no one was shot and killed. I look back at that day and think of how my life could have been taken away from me. They could have easily shot us when they rolled up on us or when we ran away but they didn't. I am very grateful that it wasn't my time to go yet. My destiny is still yet to be fulfilled.

HOW IT ALL STARTED

I got into rap when I was 16 years old, but I started dabbling when I was like 14. My brother, Nell, had a best friend that he always hung out with. He would always come around my granny's house. Therefore, he and I got really close and built a strong friendship. We became brothers for life. We got even closer when I got a little older and started being out by myself. When we first got together I was singing. We would sit up in the room and create music together. We collaborated on music for many years. He would rap and I would sing the hooks. He saw my music abilities and encouraged me to do something with my talent. Eventually, I tried to write a rap. Once I did, I never stopped. Rap became my passion. I drowned myself with learning and teaching myself how to create lyrics.

Unfortunately, he got into some trouble and was fatally shot in an altercation in Virginia. Although, his life was cut short his dream is alive in me. His death inspired me to write even more. He would want me to continue to write and pursue being the rapper that he knew was in me all along.

Music is very important to me. When I hear music or a certain beat it helps me to unlock places in my mind that I completely forgot about. It unlocks good and bad memories that I thought would never come back up. When that happens, it helps me to deal with the memories and not struggle to relive certain moments in my life.

I love being a poet and having the ability to play with words. For me, it was never about the money and the fame. Yes, all that is nice, but I genuinely love to do music. That's what keeps me going...the music. I thought that if I could write I would escape the pains and struggles of life. Truth is, there was no escaping it. The only way to escape something is to accept it and go through it. I had to live it each and every day of my life until things worked out and changed for me.

In high school, I was really reserved. I hated going to school. I would always hear my mom say, "Rell, is smart he just don't want to do the work." Since, I had to be there, I tried to make the best out of it.

I knew this guy named Y.C. We were in concert choir together. We were just playing music and voice recordings back and forth to each other. Later, he introduced me to a guy named Joe, who was a music producer. Joe and I had a close relationship from the very first time we met. From then on, we've been rocking ever since.

For the first two years of high school I played basketball. Over the summer, I dislocated my knee and tore my meniscus. Therefore, I couldn't play basketball the next year. I got really depressed because I couldn't play. I worked excessively at rehab to get my knee where it needed to be so that I could play again. When tryouts came around again I went and tried out. When I tried out I still had my knee brace on. I thought that my knee was well enough, but I didn't make the team. When I didn't make the team I got really depressed and didn't want to do nothing. Joe pushed me to make moves.

"Yo, you are not about to just sit around," he said. He literally popped up and pulled me out the house and said, "Let's go."

I'm glad I had him and other people around to help me. I had a dream to play in the NBA, but when I couldn't play sports anymore, I really leaned on music and sat and wrote. At that time, I didn't even know I was into music as much as I was. I didn't see myself doing music and taking it seriously. "It just kinda happened...it just fell in my lap." My focus shifted and I discovered a talent that I didn't know was actually my first love.

My mom bought me my first headset that looked like a McDonald's speakerphone. I would literally sit in the room for days at a time and just write music. It was terrible. The quality was terrible and nobody ever heard it except for my mom and my Aunt Quetta. That's how a lot of rappers start out. They lock themselves in a room for hours and hours and write terrible music that no one ever hears. Later, they look back at the stuff that they've originally written and ask themselves, "How in the world did I come up with this crazy stuff?" But yet, they can look back and see their progress and where they came from.

Joe became my right hand man. He is my producer, business partner, engineer...he pretty much does everything. I've known him for almost 9 years. I look forward to taking this journey with Joe and the rest of our creative team. I would say that we have written about 4,000-5,000 songs from the first time I started out to this day. I've recorded more stuff than I even remember. I've written more music than I even put out. I create stuff just by playing around with music. When I first started, I was writing nonstop. I'm not sure if we would ever go back and recreate projects that we've done in the past. For the most part, we like to create from scratch to constantly make stuff better. Music is constantly changing and so are the desires of the audience. I've put together about 8 projects and plan to do more.

Hip Hop

Everybody has that "thing" that they're good at or their "go to thing" that helps them unwind and gets their creative juices flowing. Hip hop to me is my form of art; it's my form of poetry; it's my form of basketball; it's my form of painting; it's my form of sewing. Anything that people have a passion for...anything that they love...that's what music is to me. Basketball was my "thing" until my knee injury changed that. While recovering, a new "thing" found me. Ever since then, there was nothing else that could fulfill that void. If I couldn't do music anymore I don't think I could do anything else. I put everything into my craft and I don't think I have space to find or to have another passion. I've been grinding in the music business far longer than people really know. Will Smith stated, "Why have a plan B? All plan B does is take away from plan A. You should be focusing on putting all your energy into plan A." I live by this. That's why I put my all into the one plan that I have. Music.

WORKING FOR THE MAN

I worked for the local cable company for a couple of years. With my charm and charisma, it wasn't hard to make a lot of sales and earn bonuses. I was making good money. But, the problem with that job was it wasn't fulfilling. Every time I made a sale, I thought to myself, *I am so much bigger than this. There are so many things that I can do and there is so much talent that I have in me.*

After working for the cable company, I moved to New York for a year to try to do music. While I was up there I was working for another local cable company. I came back because it was hard to be away from my kids for long periods of time and going back and forth was too expensive. I was getting into the mix and meeting a lot of people in the industry, but as far as income goes, it wasn't making sense for me to be out there.

When I came back from New York, I worked at Verizon for a short time. I couldn't function. Being at another job was depressing. Every day I went in I felt like it was a dark cloud. It's just not for me and I couldn't wrap my head around it. I was working for Verizon, a hotel, and driving for Uber all at the same time. Every day that

I got behind the wheel of my car to pick up a customer to drive them to their destination I became more and more miserable. *There has to be more to life than the everyday hustle and everyday struggle,* I would tell myself. I went from working for the cable company in New York; to working for a credit card company; to working for another credit card company; to working for another utility company all in a month. I know it sounds crazy, but I was miserable. I could like the people and I could like the job, but a week into training, I would get that feeling that I get when I'm being led to do something else. In certain situations, a feeling comes over me letting me know that it wasn't the place for me. Everywhere I worked I would feel the same way. I'm not meant to be a caged bird I'm meant to be free. I would always find myself daydreaming or I would be antsy when I would try to work a regular job.

I would tell myself, *Look, I can't do this. I have to do something else. I have to do what I love to do.* One time, when that feeling came upon me I immediately acted upon it.

"I need to talk to you," I said as I walked into my supervisor's office. "I'm leaving, I quit."

"You putting in your two week's notice?" he asked.

"Nah, I'm done."

"You're crazy."

"I know. I'm fine though. I'm going to be alright because I know where I'm supposed to be."

People would tell me, "You're crazy, you should go to school or you should stay with this company because you can move up and eventually make good money."

I'm sorry, I don't want that. The only thing that made me happy was being home with my kids or doing music. I don't want 30 or 40 years of making somebody else's dream come true. I would rather make $30,000 a year and make music than to make $100,000 doing a job that I'm wasting my brain on. I crave music each and every day. It's something that I do well. When one job didn't work out I would switch to the next one. I don't like the whole "I'm your boss" thing. I look at them as somebody who's getting paid more than me to oversee somebody else's company.

People work all day long at a job that they hate just to bring home enough money to be poor. They work their lives away on a job that takes them away from their families and the things they really desire to do in life. Why? Because they have to pay "the man." Now, don't get me wrong, if you don't mind working a job from 9 to 5 every day and you enjoy what you do, I'm not knocking that. I'm speaking to those who work every day knowing that life is passing them by while they are doing something that they hate. Just work, work, work... nonstop. It's an unfulfilling feeling to lay your head down at night knowing that you had to do what you had to do rather than being satisfied in life.

I've worked many jobs to support my family and to invest in my music. I've invested thousands of dollars a month into it. I would work my hands to the bone to support my children and my career. There were no hours too long that I could work to make sure they had what they needed. Not only was I working two and three jobs, but I was also putting myself through college to better myself. I started out going to Wilmington University, then Strayer University, and then back to Wilmington University. I majored in accounting and marketing. I plan to go back and finish my college education at some point. I'm going back because marketing is a tool that I'm going to need with owning businesses. It'll be good to do things myself without always having to rely on somebody else. Another reason why I have to go back is because it's another one of those things...if I don't finish, what kind of example am I setting? Not only for my kids but for other kids that I'm trying to inspire.

On top of working and going to school I would spend the whole night into the wee hours of the morning in the studio putting lyrics together, laying down tracks, and creating beats. That's the thing that I absolutely love to do. Rap...that is my passion that is my calling. I hunger, thirst, and crave to rap to rhyme...whatever you want to call it, but that's what I long for. No matter how many hours I spent in the studio I would get right back up the next morning to hustle to pay "the man." I've been grinding for a long time. I grind because I know that a brighter day is coming one day...someday. Maybe not today, but definitely one day. I hope...I believe...I pray.

Fear

My biggest fear in life is not living up to my full potential. I have this thing about failing that scares me. Maybe it's because of my past and my fear of going back there. That fear keeps me pushing the more...pushing to the next level. There is always room for me to constantly be better. I can constantly push towards new goals. What I consider failing is letting my talent and my brain go to waste. I feel like I will be a failure if I were to work at a regular job and not use the gifts and abilities that God has given me. I was put here to make a difference in people's lives. I want to change people's lives and to be the best at whatever I'm doing.

Every day I strive to be the best "me" that I can possibly be. I once heard Steve Harvey say that everybody has one thing in common. One thing that's exactly the same, and that is 24 hours. The thing that makes the 24 hours different is what we do with it. Your current 24 hours should be geared towards making the future 24 hours better. Meaning, grind today for a better tomorrow. Therefore, every day I have to push forward to try to be better than I was the day before.

Another thing that's constantly on my mind is being careful. I think about death a lot. Everything I do I think to myself, *What if I don't come back home to my kids?* That plays a big factor in my decision making in where I go and what engagements to take. I look at where it is and the surroundings. I'm training myself not to get so caught up in worrying about dying and enjoy life and living in the moment.

DOING MY OWN THING

I feel like people read too much into religion. Religion can be something that really pushes people away. They try to force things on people and I don't really agree with it.

I believe in God. I talk to God every day. I know that everything that I do is only possible because of Him. I don't think that you have to go to church in order to have a relationship with God. I believe that you can have a relationship with God anywhere.

If it's just one God, then what are we all divided for? That's something that I could never understand. Therefore, I just decided to do my own thing. I try to get my own understanding. I try to read deeper into the Word. Even if I go to church and listen to somebody preach, I'll try to get that underlying message. I teach my kids about God and I teach them how to pray. For me, it's more of a personal thing. I'll go and sit by the water and meditate. I can sit in His presence and not say a word; it's just a feeling for me more than anything. Everything that I do and every move that I make is based off of feelings. If I know I have to go somewhere and I'm sitting up at

3 or 4 in the morning, I know that 9 times out of 10 it's God speaking to me. I will be up feeling as if something is telling me not to go.

Once I started going back to church and started reflecting on myself I had to realize that just because people make mistakes in their lives doesn't mean they can't turn their lives around. Therefore, I try not to judge people by what they did beforehand.

My church and Apostle has always been supportive and shown love. They've never judged me because of the type of music that I make. That's big for me in general. I haven't been there as much because there has been so much going on and they understand that.

Influences

There are a lot of things that people in the industry do that people don't see. Drake just gave away a million dollars to random people and Puff has done things also. When we start doing stuff like that we want it documented because there's a stigma attached to rap artists. Everybody thinks that since you're showing that you're giving back you're just doing it for the attention, and that's not it. Why don't I have the right to show it?

If I could perform with anybody in the world it would be Jay-Z or Lauryn Hill. Creatively, Lauryn Hill is everything. Not too many people other than her and Nas can put together pieces of art the way they did and stamp it into history. Jay-Z is my biggest rap influence for the simple fact of where he came from. We both share a similar story. When he was trying to get into the industry everybody told him no. Every label company said no, so he started his own company. For me, that is one of the biggest underdog stories in music. Everybody shut their doors on him. Just like Jay-Z, when people told me no, I started my own company. We've invested our own money into promotion and building a studio. The first mixtape that we put out was called Welcome to the Machine, which I ended up taking down. Then, I released Heart of a God in 2012. After that, I released II Tickets II Fame in 2013. Next, it was Dare II Dream. I have big dreams that I am trying to put into action. My dream is to be as influential as my idol, Jay-Z. He is an incredible rapper and he has my respect. To be able to really impact people's lives; to get respect as an artist from everywhere; to get respect from CEOs of Fortune 500 companies and politicians; and just being a respectable figure that's able to make people move to get things done is amazing.

"I want to be able to use that type of power to change lives."

TRYING TO MAKE
THINGS HAPPEN

When I first moved to New York I signed with D-Teck Management, who is a part of Konvict Music. When we first started out I did a lot of coast to coast showcase shows. On September 5, 2014, I was featured in the Delaware News Journal when I was signed to Konvict music. It outlined my desire to be the next upcoming artist seeking the attention of a major label. "I was sending my music anywhere I possibly could until we got a response from a few people in their camp that heard my music." I did a few press outlets and had other engagements, but after my contract ran out we separated. Things just didn't work out. In between times, I did shows in D.C, Connecticut, New York, and Baltimore. I didn't do many shows in Wilmington, my hometown, because there weren't many outlets. Most of the venues were shut down because people didn't know how to act.

No Sugar Coating

My Aunt Quetta was my biggest supporter. She helped me the most to get where I am today. She gave me the biggest push. When she got established after finishing culinary school, I stayed at her house for months at a time. I stayed at her house because I wanted to escape my environment. I wanted to get away from the city. I had so many things going on mentally that I needed an outlet. I needed some place to go where I knew I would be safe and wouldn't get into any trouble. When I was at her house I didn't have to worry about fighting nobody and I was able to walk around the neighborhood at night and not feel like I had to keep looking over my shoulder every second. The friends that I made up there would take me in there million dollar homes to see all that they had and to meet their families. By them doing that it allowed me to see what I could have. It gave me something to keep going for. Whenever I was back in my own city I would go to the expensive neighborhoods near A. I. Middle School, pop on my headphones, and just walk and look at the expensive homes. I would say to myself, *One day I'm going to buy me one of these houses. Why not? If they can have it why can't I?* Seeing what others had motivated me to work even harder. I knew that I could have the same thing too. That motivation is going to get me where I want to be in life. It wasn't just the aspect of having a beautiful house. The whole environment was completely different. It was clean, I could breathe, there was no trash on the ground, and people speak to you…It's a whole different world out here than what we're used to. This type of mentality helped me not to get brainwashed in the mindset that a lot of people in the city have. People have no drive because they think that they're stuck and they will never go anywhere. If you feed yourself that negativity, then it will become a part of your everyday thinking and will be your life. I was sharing my dreams with this guy one time and he pretty much shot me down.

"I want to be a rap star," I told him.

"You should have smaller goals so that you don't disappoint yourself."

"What? Why would I even think like that?" I said in a disappointed but shocking voice.

It literally messed me up and I started thinking, *maybe he's right. Maybe I should just keep working and be a family man.* I had a job making almost $70,000 a year, and for a minute there, he had me thinking like him. I almost got trapped in that mindset, but I knew I wasn't built like that. Rick Ross said in his interview that people should be unlimited to dream how they want to dream and not to let anybody predetermine your future, and I believe that. To some, my dream might seem unattainable. But, others have done it, so it's definitely possible. If I would have listened to that guy's logic to submerge myself in work it would have worked for me for a short period of time before I became miserable. I would be living a very unhappy life. My life would be miserable because I would be living according to the gospel of other people. Ever since I was younger, more recently since I've been in church, people always told me that I am the lender and not the borrower. I heard that everywhere I went and that sticks with me because I believe it.

Aunt Quetta was the one that heard every single song from the beginning of my career. She would give me her honest opinion on whatever I did. Her constructive criticism that she gave pushed me to get better. Instead of her saying, "Yeah, this is good, this is dope, or you should keep going." She would say, "This is what you need to fix, this is good, this is terrible, or you need to get better at this." It was brutal honesty, but it was what I needed to really continue to push myself. She didn't chop me down to the point where I wanted to quit. She helped me to be a better writer and to step out of the box and challenge myself. Everybody needs an Aunt Quetta in their lives to be brutally honest and to give them a push to work harder and strive to be the best at whatever they do.

THE TURNING POINT

All these years of grinding towards my goal...I wanted things to happen fast. For 6 months straight I would get discouraged when things wasn't taking off like I wanted it to.

"I need it to happen now...it's not happening...we're not moving...nothing's happening," I said.

As soon as I relaxed and told myself we gotta do what we do and just take it one day at a time and breathe, things opened right up for me. It was like God was saying, "Are you done crying now?"

There was a singing competition show called The Four with P. Diddy, DJ Khaled, Meghan Trainor, and Charlie Walk that I heard about. I initially found out about the show through Instagram. Diddy and his team was posting that they were looking for rappers and singers to audition for the show. I saw the posting for like a week straight.

I just brushed it off and said to myself, *I'm not doing it because it's a show just for singers and since there are so many people submitting their music I don't think they would ever see mine. So, I* put it off for a week. It seemed like every single time I opened up my social media it was the first thing I saw.

I really battled with the decision whether to submit my information or not. I prayed about it and I still didn't know what to do. Sometimes when you pray, God doesn't give you an answer right away. It came to the point where I had to make a decision. Again, I never thought in a million years that I would be the one chosen because I knew that they had thousands of submissions from other talented artist. My submission tape was like a needle in the haystack. The decision woke me up out of my sleep about 3 or 4 a.m. I couldn't stop thinking about the show. And then, I heard a voice say to me, "Submit for the show...now." I feel like that was confirmation for me to go ahead and enter the contest. I felt as though it was a nudge...enough of you thinking about this just do it. I'm showing you this for a reason. Sometimes God speaks in a loud voice and sometimes He speaks in a small still voice.

Later that morning when I woke up that was the first thing that I did. I submitted two videos of me rapping. From there, I filled out a questionnaire, then I just waited. The process was quick for me. Everything happened in about a week. Two days later after I submitted my videos one of the casting people from the show called me. They said they think I have potential but they needed me to censor my lyrics so that the producers will know that I'm able to be on television. So, I censored my lyrics and resubmitted more videos. The producers called me the next day and said that they liked me and wanted to fly me out to LA. I started going through the audition process, but I didn't tell anybody because I didn't think I was going to make it. I didn't even tell my producer, Joe, until they told me they were going to fly me out to LA.

"Yeah, I'm about to go to LA because I submitted for that show...Diddy's show," I say interrupting our conversation about something completely different.

Joe looks at me with a puzzling look because he has no idea

what show I'm talking about. "What are you talking about?" he asks.

"You know the jawn that's been on Instagram? I sent them a post."

"Why didn't you tell me about it?"

"I don't know. I didn't think I was going to make it."

I was supposed to fly to LA, but I ended up not hearing anything for another week. I reached back out to see if I was still in consideration or not. The producer said yes and sent me my flight information. I flew out the next day. Once I got to LA there was another round of auditions. I had to audition in front of Laurieann Gibson, one of the world's most creative choreographer, and a bunch of other producers on the show. They loved me! It was like 15 people in the room and they all said, "Yes." Out of the four people that was in my group I was the only one that got picked. It all just lined up for me.

While they were still piecing everything together for the show I came back home. We were really wrestling with the contract because they basically had creative control and they get a piece of everything you do. We were unsure about it because we already had our own thing going on and we had a two year plan of what we wanted to follow.

I called Joe one day and said, "Listen, this is the biggest opportunity we've had thus far and I don't want to miss it because we're overthinking it."

"Well, what are we going to do, bro?" he asked.

"I don't want to miss my blessing by not trusting and not having faith."

"Forget it, just do it and we will handle it later," he says indicating that if we get stuck in a contract we will deal with it when we cross that bridge. "For right now, we're not going to do anything else anyway, but stay in the same position."

After I flew back to LA, The Four had to submit me to the

network to see which episode I was going to be on. I came back home after they told me I was going to be on episode 2. That same week I flew back out to LA and we started the process of making songs and doing rehearsals and stuff. It was tough for me because I couldn't bring any music or beats from home. I had thousands of songs I could have picked from, but I couldn't use it. They gave me songs that I had to pick from. I had to write lyrics to the music they gave me. It's possible to take a previously written song and put it to different music but I don't like to do that. It doesn't have the same feel to it. So, I had to start fresh and write new stuff. In order to meet their deadline, I didn't have very much time to pick a song. I worked day and night writing lyrics. I wrote 8 songs in 48 hours before we started stage rehearsals. We finally picked the beats and the music. I performed two of them on the first episode I aired on the show. I was originally supposed to be on episode 2, but when the girl challenged the rapper, I got pushed out because we ran out of time and was set to go on the next week. That was really a blessing because in every episode there are 10 people left backstage that don't get a chance to perform because of time. These people made it through the same audition process as I did. They ended up being sent home. On that particular episode it was about 8 of us that didn't get to perform. All of them was sent home except for me. They were all singers except for Nick, who was another rapper. I don't know why I wasn't sent home, I don't know why they picked me, but I'm happy that I stayed.

Before they told me that I was going to stay I was really upset because I thought I was going home.

I was like, "Man, I did all of this and I didn't even get a chance to go on. I just want to go home."

I was told to go back to my hotel room and I would be told about my travel information. About 1 am they told me that they were going to keep me for another week. During that week of waiting I just spent time writing and meditating. When I came back to film on that Thursday I already had my songs prepared for what I was going to do for that week. We did vocal coaching, stage rehearsals, wardrobe, makeup, and ran through the entire show, which took about 6-7 hours. That was really hard considering I was still on east coast time. My body never caught up.

My first day of rehearsal and my first day on stage Laurieann was in the back and she screamed, "No more Uber rides!" Indicating that my music will one day take me far and I will no longer have to continue to be an Uber driver. Those are the things that stood out to me from the whole experience.

I'll never forget that one night when my entire life changed. It was the turning point in my career. The moment I had been working towards and grinding for. And now, the floodgates of Heaven were being opened unto me. I always knew that one day things would fall in place for me, but it was that one night when things seemed to happen overnight.

THE FOUR

It's now the day that we record the show for when it airs on television. Before I went out I was watching them talk to the crowd on the monitors backstage. I was so nervous that my hands were shaking. *No time for nerves. This is the moment that I've been preparing for,* I thought. Before it was time for me to go out they played my introduction recording of my life.

"My name is Rell Jerv, I'm 24 years old, and my genre is rap. I really was exposed to rap when I was around 14 years old because a close friend of mine was a rapper at the time. My relationship with Dakee is similar to Biggie and Diddy. You have that big brother that comes along and says, 'Yo, you have talent so let's do something with it.' Unfortunately, he got into a little bit of trouble and was killed in an altercation. Like, that was my brother so..." *I start to get a little emotional and wipe the tears from my eyes.* "I'm not just doing this for me...you know what I mean? Him passing away just lit a fire under me. I have two young kids. I have to keep going for them and provide the life for them that I didn't have. I love my kids to death, so this is everything to me. When you see me walking down the street I'm a father of two but when you see me on stage I'm a completely different animal, and I feel sorry for anybody that's standing in my way."

I was headed to the stage. I walked up the steps, through a tunnel, and the doors automatically opened. I'm focused, excited, and nervous all at the same time. I feel a rush of energy that hit my whole body. The feeling is indescribable. As I'm approaching the stage I instantly connect with the audience. The crowd was so live that it was easy to feel alive. It was a good thing that the crowd was so energetic because I was the first performer of the night and I had to set the bar. On some of the episodes they changed the order of how the performers would perform, but on that particular episode I performed first.

"His energy is on fire!" says DJ Khaled, one of the judges.

I hear someone in the audience yell, "Yeah, you better walk out here like a superstar!" And, instantly all of my nervousness was gone. It only took that one person to shake that nervous feeling. Diddy is the first out of the four judges to speak.

"Peace King, how are you?"

"I'm good, I'm good."

"What's your name?"

"My name Rell Jerv."

"Where you from?"

"I'm from Wilmington, Delaware."

"What's your musical style?"

"Uh, well I rap... uh."

"Oh, you a hip hop artist?"

"Oh yeah, I'm hip hop all the way." *Cheers.* "Yeah, I heard y'all calling." *Smiling.*

"How does it feel being a hip hop artist knowing that if you get through to the next phase that you'll have to challenge somebody that's a singer?"

I feel like it would be challenging if I would advance to the next round because I would be battling more singers. But, I just looked at it as a competition because I have two kids to take care of. They depend on me and it's my job to make sure they have what they need. Therefore, I can't allow what looks like a stumbling block to get the best of my thoughts and hinder me. I'm going to perform as if I was performing against a platform full of rappers.

"I feel like that's a tough challenge, but at the end of the day I'm here to do what I got to do and my kids gotta eat… so this ain't no game for me."

"Heyyyyyy," Meghan, another judge says.

"That's right, that's right," DJ Khaled says.

Diddy pretends to eat out of a bowl, which cues the audience to chant.

"Eat, eat, eat," they chant over and over again. That's his slogan for this show…eat. He is looking for artists that are hungry for success and will stop at nothing to get it.

"God bless you and good luck," he says to me.

"Yeah," I say with confidence.

"Let's get it."

When I was on stage and my music started to play I felt the biggest rush that I have ever felt in my life. I was blank. I closed my eyes for a second to just feel the music…and I was just gone from there. My body felt like I had grown the size of a giant; my hands felt like I was about to do a lyrical kung fu as I orchestrated my fingers to the beat; my tongue was burning like a furnace as I spat fire. What I'm trying to say is that I tuned into a beast. A beast that I knew was there, but yet, a beast that I'd never seen before. This is the greatest feeling that I have ever felt. The lights were shining, the music was playing, and the fans were screaming…I was in my element. Oh yeah, right here on stage, is where I belong. This is greatness. This is what I was created for. There is nothing else in the world that I would rather be doing.

It appeared that I was looking at the judges during my

performance. Truth is, I was looking into the cameras at the millions of viewers watching from their homes. I was given this tip backstage while being "Boom Kacked" by the original boom kacker herself Laurieann Gibson. She told me that when I have my stance and when I'm giving it to them I have to make the people at home feel what I was giving because they are the ones that were going to be my followers. I was so zoned out at connecting with the audience and trying to reach the viewers through the cameras that I only can see the judges just a little bit. There was no doubt in my mind that I had the judges hooked from the first line of my rap after the beat dropped. I quickly glance at them. They are so serious. Not many emotions...just a hard stare with a head bob. They made it really hard for me to read what was going through their minds. But, it was quite obvious that I was entertaining them the way they bobbed their heads to the beat. All I wanted to do was do my thing and unleash the beast as I impressed the judges. The crowd loved every moment of my performance. Thank goodness! A good crowd really makes a difference in a performance. Their energy is very important because they don't know anything about you. So, the most important thing is to get them from the beginning if you can. When the crowd is hyped it makes it easier to feed off their energy to create a more powerful performance. But, no matter how great of a performance you give and no matter how much you are doing you will always find that one person that's not feeling your performance. You can ask any performer how they always catch the eye of that one person. It can either mess you up or you can just keep riding the wave. Luckily, everybody was so into my performance that they just kept feeding me energy.

YEP, I'M THE BOMB

I finally finish my first performance. The judges are clapping and the audience is cheering. I am smiling with confidence because I know I rocked the house. I feel really good and I can't wait to hear what the judges are going to say about my performance.

"Oh my God, I love him," Meghan says to Diddy.

"Meghan," the host calls out so she could give her critique.

"I love especially when rappers come out and you can actually hear every single word...and you can tell they have amazing breath control. And there were so many special moments that you created and wrote and you can see that as a songwriter. I love when you said, 'Live it, live it.' That was so sick. I would like to see you loosen up a little bit."

"I got you," I say hinting to her that I can make whatever changes are necessary.

"But it was so clever and so talented," she continues.

"I got you, thank you," I say again.

"Yeah."

"Charlie!" the host shouts to the other judge to give his critique.

"Yeah, I was just thinking about Hip Hop's the number one genre...the number one most consumed genre."

"Biggest in the game," DJ Khaled chimes in.

"Real artist do what you just did... and you did you," Charlie concludes.

"Thank you, thank you."

There was a lot of feedback that all of the judges gave that the viewers at home didn't get a chance to see because the show had to be edited for the time restraints to air the show on television.

"Khaled," the host says to the next judge.

"What's one of your favorite rap artist?" he asks.

"Um, somebody I studied the most is Jay." *Cheers.* "But I feel like I take stuff from everybody. I take stuff from Kendrick...even the new guys. I take whatever I can to better myself." *Cheers.*

"Diddy," the host says to the final judge.

"The thing that I didn't really like is...if I can detect the influences too much of other people." *Boos.*

My countenance changes. I am listening but I don't agree with what he is saying. The thing with music is there nothing new under the sun. *Everybody picks from somewhere, everybody starts from somewhere. Everybody has their favorite artist and takes from them and puts their own twist on it.* Although I'm influenced by other artists I have my own style. I do me, and I wanted Diddy to know that.

Diddy continues, "But the thing that I loved was like 35 seconds...into it...I heard Rell. I heard you." I am uplifted again and it shows on my face. Yes! I wanted him to hear me and not my idols. *Cheers.*

"Loosen up...whew," Meghan says. She squirms around in her seat to loosen her shoulders. I copy her with a smile on my face.

"Loosen up baby. Yeah!" Diddy shouts with a smile on his face.

"I like that jacket too," I say hoping he would give me his expensive jacket.

"You like my jacket?"

"I told them I wanted to trade with you but they said that you wasn't going to have that."

"Yo, check this out...after the show, I can make anything happen my name is Diddy." *Cheers and laughter.*

The rest of the judge's critiques were edited out for timing purposes. DJ Khaled asked me, "Can you see your song up and playing in rotation with the Jay-Z, Drake, or J-Cole songs?"

It is now time for the four panelist to put my performance to a vote to see if it's enough challenge one of the four other contestants for their seats. Surrounding me was the four rings that represent the panelists. If they vote "Yes" the ring will turn blue and if they vote "No" the ring will turn red. In order to challenge one of the other contestants I would need all four rings to be blue. If one of them turns red I am automatically sent home. After a few moments, which seemed like an eternity of waiting the host announced that they were ready to reveal the judge's votes. All eyes were on me...at home and at the venue.

THE VERDICT

"The verdict is in," she says. "Let's see if the panel thinks that you deserve to challenge one of the four."

The first ring turns blue. "One yes, it's a blue that's a yes." The second ring turns blue. "Blue! Two blues, two yeses." The third ring turns blue. "Number 3, three yeses! One more and we have our first challenge of the night. Come on Rell...are we doing this?"

Diddy takes off his shades and gives "the stare" that he always gives that causes his eyes to twinkle.

"Four yeses, it's a challenge!!!" she shouts.

"Ohhh!" I shout while shaking my head yes.

The crowd is going insane. Diddy stands up and does the "eat" motion and the audience begin to chant.

The Challenge

Since I made it to the next round I am given the opportunity to choose one of the other four contestants to challenge to take their seat. I think they already had the order of performers that they wanted to go in, but once people started to challenge the order changed. The question of the night is who I would like to challenge? I think that everyone probably thought that I would challenge Jason because he was the only other male that was up there. I pretty much already knew who I was going to challenge if I had the opportunity.

"It's only right for me to take out who took out the rapper and that is Cheyenne."

I know for sure that the audience and the judges didn't see that one coming.

Cheyenne had to perform first but it was up to me to see if I could top her performance. Then, the audience will decide who claims a seat and who goes home.

By the time I went for the second performance the audience was already in. They had already made their minds up after the first song. Then, I felt like I can really calm down and swag it out. At one point, everybody was just looking around like...what is this? But, by the time I was halfway through it was undeniable.

Once my nerves left me...I was gone...I was in the zone. I didn't feel anything. I had the audience locked right where I wanted them. I even messed up and got back on track without anybody even knowing. I fumbled on the flow on one part, but I caught it. A lot of people didn't notice it until they went back and replayed it. I went from locking eyes with the judges, engaging with the audience, to approaching my opponent from a distance. I made sure she knew that I was there to take her seat and to claim my spot. The very last line in my rap I said, "Don't get stuck in this moment cause I own it," and the sirens went off. The crowd and the judges goes wild. Everybody is standing on their feet and screaming their heads off. My opponent throws a snare at me and looks towards the judges. She already knew her spot was taken before the judgment even took place. This was the most electrifying performance that

I have ever delivered. It felt like fire running through my veins. Somebody really should have called the bomb squad because I just blew the stage up! Or maybe, they should have called the fire department because I set the mic on fire!

Who goes? Who stays?

It is now time for the judges to give their opinions on our performances. The way the crowd responded I already knew I had this performance in the bag. Diddy was the first to speak. I'm glad he spoke first because I felt like his opinion mattered the most and his opinion persuades the way the other judges respond.

He said, "Rell, you really, really excited me." To hear Diddy say my name was pretty dope. Just to know that I could move such an icon like him was an honor.

After all the judges told us individually about our performance the two of us are standing side-by-side waiting for the audience's votes to be calculated. My heart is pumping so fast and thumping so hard that I thought it was going to jump out of my chest and fall on the stage. It wasn't because I was nervous about the final decision. It was simply because I knew this was my moment. *I knew that my turn had finally come for the world to know who I am. I'm Rell Jerv baby, and if you don't know you better ask somebody!* Fergie snaps me out of my thoughts.

"Ladies and gentlemen, the results are in. And the winner of this competition is—" *Pause.* The audience, the judges, and the viewers at home were on the edge of their seats. It was definitely a nail biting moment. The suspense was killing everybody, especially me. *This seems like the pause of eternity. Is it me or is it Cheyenne? Come on Fergie, spit it out!* I thought to myself? Seconds later after all the audience's votes were calculated. I heard the host yell.

"Rell!" Once again, the crowd goes wild. I do a fist pump. I am smiling a smile of relief. "Rell, go and claim your seat."

Unbelievable

The way that I became known over night was incredible. People from all over the world from all walks of life was in to my music. Young, old, male, female, Black, White, Indian...everybody. I've even had people from Australia and Africa, and other faraway places reaching out to me. The minute after I performed people was requesting my album and asking when I will be doing a concert near their city. I was ready for fame, but I wasn't expecting it to take off as quickly as it did. I have more posts than I could read and more messages than I could even open up. My phone was blowing up and social media was simply ridiculous. I received an overwhelming response of love for both of my performances. Now, people are googling my name and seeing that I have a lot of music already out there. If I had such a mass of communication, and this is only the beginning, I don't know how I would even be able to keep up with the outpouring of responses when things really take off for me. I'm being pulled in so many directions, and I have to say that it feels really good. Even if I don't win this competition, my goal is to get worldwide recognition. Even though my journey here is not done, my mission that I sought out to do has been accomplished.

After the first show aired that week was bananas. We had to do crazy press. We were on all kinds of social media outlets and buzzing on local radio shows. I even made it back in The News Journal again back home. My family was blowing my phone up like they'd never did before. Everybody was just super excited and proud for me. I know my kids were happy to see me on television too.

WEEK TWO

It's the second week that I'm on The Four. I am so ready for this day. Last week was incredible. I definitely turned the page to the next chapter in my life. I know my fans are excited to hear more from me and I cannot wait to deliver. I have no idea what this night is going to bring, but I got my boxing gloves and I'm ready to fight.

Every week the contestants open the show with a group performance. I'm the first person to come out. It felt really good opening the show. My name was sparkling in gold lights and the audience was screaming their heads off. The energy in the room was crazy! I didn't feel like a contestant I felt like a superstar. I was basking in the presence of the spotlight.

We came out one by one and did our separate parts. The singers sang the song Finesse by Bruno Mars and I wrote my own rap to the rap section of the song. The crowd was so live that they made me feel like dancing from one side of the stage to the other. I'm not much of a dancer, but I sho nuff know how to do a two-step to a beat. Each performer came out with their own type of flare, which added more fuel to the fire. It was cool how we connected as a group during our performance. We all came out from different areas on or near the stage to make our performances more creative.

The Breakdown

The people watching at home don't see that we have breaks in between takes and the audience is completely switched out. They switch out the audience halfway through with people that don't even know anything about the show.

After I did the opening of the show I was fine. We went backstage for about an hour and they completely switched the audience out. I broke down backstage from everything that was going on. My breakdown was a combination of everything...my songs...song choices...everything. Two days before my performance I had a completely different hook that I wanted to do, but it got struck down and I couldn't do it. I wanted to use my own beats but they told me they couldn't clear them. I told them I owned the beats and I would sign over the rights, but they refused to let me use them.

"I can't do this, I can't be myself up here," I said becoming more and more upset.

I had a lot of restrictions that was making it hard for me to perform. At the end of the day I had to do what I had to do but I literally said, "I don't want to do this song. If I do this beat I'm gonna go home...they're not going to like this song." And, nobody would listen to me.

The day of the show we were recording for about 16 hours. It was an extremely long day. I got up before sunrise and had to do press all day. I didn't perform until after 10 o'clock that night. I was physically drained from prepping for the show on top of the 3 hour time difference.

Another thing that I was dealing with was that it was my brother's birthday. He passed away a few years ago and I was still dealing with it. I was feeling it even more because my cousin Dean had passed away while I was on the show. So, I was thinking about that really heavy too. To be so far away from my family at this time of grieving wasn't easy. Then, I started thinking about my kids. I had to be away from my kids for a whole month straight. Even though, I'm here doing what I have to do in order to put them in a better position, it was really hard. I was used to them running and jumping in my arms when they come home from school or if I was having a bad day. I had them go and pull Joe, my producer, and bring him backstage. There were so many emotions swarming around in me that I really didn't know how I was going to get through my performance if I had to challenge someone.

I said, "Yo, dog, I don't know what's going on. I don't know how I'm going to get through this night."

We were back there talking about it for like 30 minutes before it was time to continue taping. They are about to bring out the first contestant for the night. If that performer gets three blue rings from the panel of judges he or she will continue on to the next phase, which would be to choose a person to challenge. They don't tell us in advance who is going to come out and perform. We don't know until they announce it to everybody else. Last week, it was different because I was the challenger coming out to win a seat. Now, I am on the other side of the fence. I could potentially have my seat taken away, or I could be the one that doesn't get picked to do a challenge for this week. Even though I'm caught up in my emotions I am here to do a job. So, I'm going to do what I have to do.

WHO'S NEXT?

The next contestant is being introduced. When they first said they had a rapper I knew exactly who was coming out. Besides me, there was only one other rapper backstage. I already knew that if he made it through to the next round everybody was going to want to see a challenge between us.

Nick came out to do his thing. I didn't know what he was going to do as far as his performance. He had weeks to prepare and put his whole performance together. The rest of us had to do press and rehearsals every day and I had to write several different songs. I had to write the intro to the opening part of the show. It was a lot that had to go into that one week for us. When you're a challenger all you have to do is focus on only one thing, and that's the songs that you have. For his performance, he did an industry beat. He did a beat that everybody recognized. When the beat came on, the crowd went crazy over the song choice he used rather than what he was actually saying. The music he used belonged to one of the judges. I could have gone up there and rapped for 2 minutes but it takes something else to be able to put together an entire song. As soon as the mob beat dropped I looked at Joe and we already knew by the way the crowd reacted to the music that the energy was going to be different once I tried to do an original song if I had to challenge him. On top of that, I asked for the Bad Boys for Life music. I asked them for the beat Nick used but they wouldn't give it to me. Nick came out and performed a battle rap. He had 3 weeks to come up with the antics in his performance like approach the judges and sit on the step, which is something that I was specifically told I could not do because of camera angles and stuff. We had to remain inside the blue rings so that the cameras could pick us up.

After his performance, he got positive feedback from the judges. When it was DJ Khaled's turn to share his thoughts he immediately goes off saying he wants to see a head to head battle between Nick and me. That was fine, but the choice was supposed to be left up to Nick who he wanted to battle. Plus, Nick hadn't even made it through yet. I feel like the way DJ Khaled went off initiated the challenge up front. When I talked to Nick that night he said he wasn't going to challenge me. He was going to challenge somebody else so that it would be two rappers up there. But, it was one of those things where we had to go at it because of the position we were put in.

I'm Up

Since, Nick made it through and the challenge was presented, I have to perform first. After the break and after my challenger performed they rolled my previously recorded tape on my thoughts from last week's show and anything I wanted to say to my challenger for this week.

"Last week was pretty cool. I just was focused on impressing the judges. Hearing Diddy say my name was pretty dope. 'Rell, you really, really, really excited me.' I dreamed of having such an icon acknowledge me. 'I think Rell ceased the moment in time. Hip hop is on the rise, and he came wit it,' Diddy comments. "It feels great to be a member of the four. It's like a whirlwind...it never stops it's never a dull moment. The lyrics I wrote for this week are really geared towards the challenger and talking about how hungry I am. I have to put food on the table for my kids and set them up for the future. When I say my kids got to eat, that means you should probably step out of the way. For any challenger that's coming after my seat...I just want to say bring your A game because I'm not giving up my seat easy and you're going to have to put in some work to get it from me." *Laughs.*

My music starts off slow and I start to sing. Throughout my performance I can tell that the energy level is not as high as it was during Nick's performance. It's okay because I am still able to engage with the audience and deliver an exceptional performance considering everything that had just happened backstage and everything I dealt with these last couple of days.

When my performance was over I went back to sit in my seat.

"Did you hear me stumble?" I asked Zhavia, another contestant.

"No, no," she replied.

I see the judges whispering.

"Rell wasn't on," says Charlie.

"I know," Meghan replies.

Now it's time for Nick to challenge my performance. Right away he starts battling. I made it visually clear that I wasn't intimidated or impressed. But, it wasn't about my thoughts it was about what the audience thinks. It was up to them to decide who stays and who goes. I think the audience is more for him only because in his initial performance he did a song with music that was very popular and familiar to them. Therefore, that performance was stuck in their minds.

It is now time to see what the judges have to say. I walk down the steps from my seat to join Nick and Fergie on the stage.

Instead of her asking the judges what they thought about our performances she immediately starts talking about the breakdown I had backstage.

"Rell, backstage it's been an emotional night for you. Can you tell us why?" Fergie asks while shoving the mic in my face.

The expression that I gave wasn't because I was still feeling emotional it was because she had put me on the spot when I wasn't expecting it. *I can't believe that this is happening right now. She literally put me on the spot,* I thought.

When I was backstage they asked me twice, "Are you sure you don't want to talk about it?"

I said, "No, I'm fine, stop asking me about it." Now that I'm on stage they talk to Fergie in her headset and told her to ask me about it. And again, I said, "No, I'm fine. It's no excuse let's just get to the judging."

Then she said, "Don't you think the people would want to know?"

Personally, I didn't want to talk about again. They didn't understand when I said I didn't want talk about it, but they just kept pushing the issue. I mustered up enough strength to be able to perform so let's just leave it at that. I guess they thought if they would ask me while the cameras were rolling I would give an answer. She shouldn't have done that right before the audience voted. I wasn't trying to make the audience feel sorry for me and I wasn't trying to use a sad story to win their votes either. Everybody goes through things in life. I felt like she put me at a disadvantage by bringing it up again, but she was only doing what she was told.

Now that all eyes and cameras are on me I have no choice but to answer.

Sigh. "If you watched the first episode in here you know when I talked about my brother and my inspiration in why I got into rap, and he passed away and today is actually his birthday. So, it was an emotional moment for me backstage. But, that ain't no excuse.

Nick is great he's a tough competitor, he came with it and...you know it's in your hands now," I say. *Applause.*

"Let's hear what our panel thinks. Meghan?" Fergie says

"I think with you Nick your writing...there wasn't any hooks. We couldn't tell where the chorus was and that's something that Rell does really well, but your lyrics all together were way stronger than Rell's. Rell your story is wrapped around my heart and I just crumble with emotions for you. But, if I had to pick who to sign to a label tonight I would pick Nick."

"Thank you," Nick says.

"Charlie?" Meghan says.

"Nick, I think you're more of a poet than maybe a competitor that will end up on the four stage tonight. I do have to go with you Rell because I believe in the long run you belong up there and you have a story to tell and I know there's more in you to come."

"Thank you, thank you," I say.

"The original Bad Boy, Diddy." Meghan says."

"Aye, when I first went in the studio with B.I.G he wrote a rhyme that was like 64 bars long with no chorus. But, just like I told Biggie, I said you can keep on rapping until you're blue in the face you gon lose people man. It's about the songs."

"Absolutely, I can do that as well just to let you know," Nick chimes in.

"Rell, need you to talk to me, baby. This is love here. Talk to me. It's written all over your face, man."

"I mean...I definitely feel like I was caught up in my emotions a little bit, but that's no excuse you know what I mean? Obstacles are always going to come up, so that's something that I got to deal with." *Applause.*

"If we going to work together we have to be honest. This show is about stepping up and showing how bad you want it, and I think Nick showed that he wanted it more than you today."

"That's respectable."

"Thank you panel. Audience, please vote now."

The audience pulls out their cell phones to use as a voting device. Some are voting for me and some are voting for Nick.

"Is it going to be Rell Jerv, member of The Four? Or, Nick, our challenger?" Fergie asks.

THE OUTCOME

Since, the audience is fresh every time you have to hook them all over again for each performance. The audience is more-less for the underdog...the challenger. The audience feeds off of the judge's reactions and comments making it a bit difficult for them to form their own opinions.

I think that Nick had a better performance than mine, but again, he had more time to prepare. However, he didn't show that he was a better artist than me. Diddy even said he had a couple of good lines but he didn't show anything about him as an artist. I was very upset at how they edited my performance to make it look like it wasn't a good one. They chopped it up to the point where it looked like it didn't even make sense. If they would have let my entire performance play with all the bars and hooks I had, it would have been on fire. The types of antics Nick used in his first performance put him at an advantage because he wasn't limited to that space. I can battle rap too. But, it wasn't supposed to be a battle rap. I was given songs and I couldn't really change them. I came prepared with songs to be an artist while my opponent came to battle. So, I was like, "Ok..." The judges were saying that they only remembered the first performance. *So, my question was are y'all making a decision based on the first one or the second one that you saw? I felt as though they made the decision based on the battle part of the second performance.*

Before Fergie announced the winner I already knew Nick won. We were on stage for a while laughing and talking before all that stuff that everybody saw on tv aired. Although, the judges had split decisions it was pretty obvious who they felt should take the empty seat. The outcome was still a little puzzling to me because they had to cut out so much of Nick's performance because he pretty much completely bashed the entire show. Later they edited it to make the outcome make sense. How can you vote for somebody that is speaking against an opportunity before it's even offered?

That was a very hard moment for me considering everything that I had faced that week. I wasn't even going to make my battles public. I was not trying to use my brother's birthday as a sympathy card to win votes. What everyone failed to realize is that Fergie asked me, which I was very unhappy about. Yes, I felt myself getting caught up in my emotions, but I still did one hell of a performance. The same thing that they were trying to make an excuse for me was the same thing they were trying to give Zhavia a pass on. They were saying she had a "bad night" because she was unable to talk and had to rest her voice. But, nobody even brought that up. She might not have been able to talk but what was she going through personally in life? They even told us not to take advantage of her because she was sick. The rules should have been the same across the board for everyone.

There was more feedback that the judges gave us that was later edited out that home viewers didn't see. DJ Khaled told Nick,

"Don't play yourself, reward yourself. You won as far as battle rap. But, Rell, you came out and you put it into song form, which is what we came here to do. And, you showed that you ain't nothing to play with as far as the bars go."

Once the votes were all calculated Nick and I stood side by side waiting for Fergie to announce the winner. Just as I had figured, she called out Nick's name. Of course, I was disappointed. Who wants to be eliminated in a competition? But, my mission here was accomplished and this chapter of my life is over. It is time to turn the page of this book of life and move on to the next phase that the future holds.

"Rell, tell us how you feel?" Fergie says

"I feel good. Listen, one night does not define me as an artist. This platform just gave me all the ammo I needed to get to where I needed to get...so it's on."

It was also edited out when all the judges told me that they could tell that something was going on and that it showed in my performance.

I said, "I got a thousand songs that's ready to go right now."

"The fact that you said that I know that you're gonna be alright," Diddy responded.

Backstage he told me that he's glad I came on the show and didn't feel like I had to water down who I was. He also told me to keep hip hop alive. It felt good to have those last moments of encouragement.

Nick texted me a few days after our show aired and I asked him how he was doing? He finally experienced what I experienced as far as song choices, beats and not being able to change certain things about his music. He really got a taste of the restrictions and knows what it feels like to be on the other side and not have those weeks of preparation.

"This tv stuff is just that...tv," Nick said.

Rell Jerv

It's not easy having your hands tied when you're used to being so free with your music. When you can't do what you want to do creatively it can make you feel like you're inside of a box. Everybody thought that being eliminated was so bad, but in actuality, it's not.

AT THE END OF THE DAY

I was happy to know that I did an amazing job and pushed myself to the next level in my career. Throughout this process I challenged myself with my songwriting skills, singing abilities, and strengthened my vocals. I challenged myself in ways that I probably would not have been able to do if I did not have this experience. I was able to meet my expectations during vulnerable moments in my life and still feel like I came out on top. If I had to do it all over again I would in a heartbeat because there are a lot of valuable moments and experiences that I've walked away with that has made me a better artist.

After the elimination they rolled my exit tape as I walked off the stage.

"It's not about making excuses. He outperformed me. It's always tough when you deal with things that really hit home. At the end of the day I'm a man and I'm a father, and I'm working for all of them. I lost my seat, but that don't mean that I'm going to stop."

People was wondering why I was smiling when I lost. I didn't lose. I came out here to do what I said I was going to do. I was fine. It didn't hurt or discourage my confidence one bit because I know who I am, and I'm comfortable with that. As long as a person is comfortable in their own skin no one can ever make them feel otherwise. It's not always the person who wins that actually wins. I didn't want to be in a contract where there are so many restraints. I wouldn't have been able to do music like I wanted to do. Now, I understand why Prince wrote the word slave on his face. You have to do what you're told to do and I wanted to be able to be myself in my music.

The Other Contestants

I met Nick before we actually challenged each other. Like the other contestants, we kept in contact after the show. After my elimination he realized that the television industry is not all peaches and creams. He quickly learned that with all of the restrictions the spotlight is not all that it's cracked up to be.

I already knew Cheyenne, Jason, and Tim before we started shooting. The only person I didn't know was Zhavia. The first day that I was there I talked to and had dinner with Cheyenne, which was actually weird because we challenged each other. She was the very first person that I started to build a relationship with throughout the process. It seemed as if she was throwing a lot of shade and snares during my performance, but in reality, it was just the nature of the show. Cheyenne is a good singer. I feel like she's more in that old school lane. She's dynamic. She can do so many different things. This is stuff that we've learned by just playing around and singing. We would all just play around and have jam sessions in our hotel rooms.

Candice was like an older sister to me. She's so real and down to earth. She doesn't care about the tv aspect of it all. She's going to say whatever she wants to say and she's going to show love to whoever she wants to show love to. Away from the cameras, Candice and I had that real connection like, "What's up, sis?" The same thing with Jason. It was like, "Yo, this is my bro." I think that Candice was a good singer too. Her control is crazy. The way she can catch those runs...I never saw anybody who could do a run like that and be that clean with it. She has that old R&B swag and still be unique at the same time.

Jason is just a freak of nature. Everybody thinks that he only sings one way. His range is ridiculous. He can sing any song and make it his own. Jason and I are super cool. We talk every day. I would say that I'm closest to Jason because we are closer in age. Jason and I were the closest because we spent the most time together throughout the entire process. We became part of the four together. So, when I walked out on stage I saw Jason and we immediately made eye contact. I was like, "My boy." They even had to tell him, "You can't give your opponent a standing ovation because he's coming to challenge you." That's how tight we were.

Meghan made a comment on the previous episode allegedly comparing Jason's performance to John Legends. Apparently, Jason's feelings were hurt by that and wanted it to be made known. He approached her and sang to her. I didn't know all of that happened until I watched the episode. Everyone thought security came and escorted him off the stage when it was really the time keeper guys. I don't know their proper titles, but they're the ones that tells us when to come out, where to stand, etc. They were trying to move the time along and stay on schedule.

Tim is like the little brother. He reminds me of Michael Jackson a lot, even with the dancing. He's so unique. Although he reminds me of Michael Jackson he reminds me of himself. You can't really put your finger on it, but he has something.

All of us were so close that we would leave our doors propped open to our connecting hotel rooms. We didn't even worry about our valuables laying out in the open. You could just walk through to anybody's room. And no, no one was creeping in the middle of the night.

Although we were building a relationship we all knew what we were there for. Even at our young ages, we all had that maturity level where we were able to separate the two. That was the beauty of it. Being able to keep those friendships knowing that we were in a competition. Cheyenne and I already had that talk.

I said, "If you're up there I'm probably going to have to take you out."

She was like, "Bring it."

Although, it was more-less like trash talk, we understood that there only could be one winner. So, we had to build relationships while we were there.

I talk to everybody, including the contestants that didn't get a chance to perform, almost every day in a group chat on Instagram. We try to stay connected and continue to build a strong relationship.

Honestly, I'm not sure if Diddy would ever want to work with me in the future. I am so grateful to have been able to show my talent to someone that is so powerful in the industry. He has an amazing reach. He can work with people and introduce them to the world where they will later become superstars. Just to be given a platform to demonstrate to him and the world what I can do is awesome. To work with anybody of that stature is good, but like working with anybody, the business aspect of it would have to make sense.

MY MUSIC

I try to keep my music as genuine as possible. By doing that I draw in so many people from different demographics. I look at the traffic that comes through my social media, and I'm proud to say that I am reaching all types of people ranging in ages from 18 to 45 years old. I have even reached kids younger than that.

Everybody in rap has similarities. I'm not much of a freestyler, I don't practice that. I write when I'm inspired. I have to live in order to write. One thing about rapping is that we all have a story to tell. The way you carry yourself outside of the music on a daily basis, how people see you give back, how you interact with your fans and family sets rappers aside from other rappers. These things are huge. Along with all of those qualities, I have a sound that people haven't heard before. The first thing a lot of people say to me is, "Your voice is really something special and we've never heard a voice like that before." Then, they look into my background and they look through my social media and see how I interact with the fans. People don't usually do that. I think that's really important to interact with the crowd that's supporting you. Just a small gesture like simply "liking" their comment or post can make a big difference in someone's life. When you interact with your fans, it make people feel like they are more connected to you and it definitely draws more people. You miss a lot when you don't even try. I had kids reach out to me saying that they could never sing like other people on the show. They would tell me how much they admire and look up to me. For them to hear from me that I wasn't good in the beginning and that it just takes work encourages them to push that much harder.

I motivate through my music. The overwhelming response on social media feels good because it is helping me build a stronger complex about my music and who I am as an artist. By having a base of people who are constantly giving me feedback, I'm not guessing what the people want to hear. They'll give me the order of the things they love to hear. I am able to deliver what they want to hear, but yet, still be me. I try to create a little something for everybody. Now I have more of a guideline to go by when I'm putting together a project. If I put out a song, and it only gets 500 likes versus another song that got 5,000 likes, it's pretty obvious what type of song we will be leaning towards. It's important to listen to your audience because they're telling you what the people want and they're going to be the ones that push you to wear you need to be.

Once people invest in me and want to dig to figure out who I am outside of the music they will start to see all of the things that I've been through. Then they will say, "Wow, if you went through this and you went through that than anybody can do it." Then, when they hear my music it will start to connect. They will be able to figure out what I'm really talking about.

I feel like many people can relate to what I've been through. The everyday struggles of living in the hood, the absence of a father, and being raised by a struggling, single mom. That's what makes my music relatable. So many people have been in predicaments where they didn't know what was going to happen next, but they still had to figure out a solution. For most of us, that was our everyday life.

Life Goes On

After the show, I felt like people were accepting me and they didn't even know me. It wasn't just the music, it was the authenticity. People felt like they could reach out and touch me because they felt like they knew me. I think the reason my following got so big was because people felt close to me. They felt like it was real and not gimmicky. Being in this position has allowed me to open up more and to see more. I was so focused on where I was trying to go that what people said to me wasn't inviting and I wouldn't pay attention to them. Now, I have allowed myself to see the bigger picture.

The first performance after The Four was dope. We packed out the venue. It was awesome to get so much love in support in my own town. There were a couple hundred people that came out to support me and 4 or 5 other local artists. This show was a little different from any other show because now people really know me. People were more receptive because they saw me on television and I'm from their area.

Since I've been back from LA I got a couple of offers to work on some projects. While I work on those projects, I'm also finishing up my upcoming album called Far From Legendary that will drop later on this year. I'm working on separating from the show and networking for what's next. Even though, I was very restricted on the show with the type of music that I could do, I never changed who I was. I feel like that's one of the reasons why people gravitated towards me.

I'm really trying to separate from being Rell from The Four and going back to being my own artist and not get stuck in that world. Unfortunately, a lot of people will get stuck in that world of being just a person from the show and not their own person. I don't walk in the shadows of nothing or nobody. I let my light shine wherever I go. I had my own image before the show and I will continue to keep it after the show.

Not for Me

People keep asking me if I'm going to try out for next season or will I ever do another competition? I think I'm done with competitions. I would go if I was asked to perform or just to be a part of the audience, but not to be a contestant. I went out there and I did what I had to do and I got the following I needed to push to the next level. I left on a positive note, so now, it's just capitalizing on the business mind. I've already had some opportunities in the mix that presented itself. It's just a matter of making the right moves at the right time. You can't be too quick to jump because everything that looks good is not good for you.

PURSUIT TO HAPPINESS

I encourage everyone to follow their dreams. The biggest thing for me was timing. Things didn't happen when I wanted them to and they didn't happen when I thought they would. Things started to unfold when I was fully in a position to receive them. Patience is a virtue.

Sometimes a person can get discouraged when they have put in so much time and they're not getting recognized for what they really can do. I was motivated by everybody else to keep working towards the dream. Many times I wanted to quit but everybody else saw potential in me. Everybody that invested time and their hard earned money in me kept pushing me not to give up. I always had in the back of my mind if I gave up now what would tomorrow bring…I would never know. I don't like regrets. I hate to have to think back and ask myself, *Man, what if I would have done this or what if I would have just put out one more song? Or, what if I would have went to this place or event?* I once heard a saying that people give up right before they make it. That's the one thing that kept pushing me forward. I told myself, *I can't give up now. I've already started...I can't give up now.* After I had my kids, I asked myself, *if I gave up how are they supposed to think that they can fight through any obstacle if they saw me give up? How am I supposed to preach to the choir if I haven't even done it?*

First off, you can't be afraid to put in the time to invest in yourself. Whether that investment is going to school and learning, perfecting your craft, or making financial investments. Secondly, make small attainable goals. Our first goal was to make a good song...make something that was of a good quality. From there, let's try to put together a project. Once that was achieved, the next goal was to create a project that we can put out to people and get feedback from. We recorded for three years before we even put out a song. Just perfecting the craft. From the day Junior, another person in my production team, sent me his first beat, he has gotten so much better. I encouraged him to try new stuff and not just what was already out here. I told him to push himself to try different genres of music and now his versatility is crazy.

Changing Lives

I want to get to a level where I can take care of my family and change lives. I don't want to be known as someone that just take, take, take. I want to change lives by helping and giving back to my community.

I see a single mom on the bus with three kids that has to wake up at 5 in the morning. I ask myself, "How can I make a difference in a life like that?" Another one of my ultimate goals is to do something with the homeless and be more hands on rather than just giving money to somebody.

It's hard to figure a solution to the outcry of the community. It's going to take more than one person to figure it out because it's a situation that has been spinning out of control for such a long time.

"You have to start so young and it's going to take so long because it's hard to change the mindset of an adult."

We want to invest in quality, affordable apartment complexes that will help make living easier. Not so we can generate income but to help the community. Rent is ridiculously expensive and housing is of poor quality. People have to choose a quality apartment that they cannot afford or an affordable slum in a neighborhood that their kids are unable to go outside and play. At my complex, people would be paying rent, but the money would be reinvested back into the property. Tenants would be paying to keep up and maintain the complex. We wouldn't be making any profit from it.

A lot of times people just want somebody that understands and somebody to acknowledge their struggles. Even if it's not financially, just showing your presence and listening to somebody talk, or just making them smile can make a difference. Sometimes a listening ear is all that people search for. I am positioning myself to one day be able to change people's lives on every scale. I know that it won't be easy, but I am up for the challenge.

MISSION INCOMPLETE

Just like I said in my final words on The Four, "One night doesn't define me as an artist." This dream that I have...the world didn't give it and the world can't take it away. The elimination did not hurt my career one bit. I've been writing music longer than people even realize and I'm not about to stop now. As a contestant, I wasn't able to be myself and show the world all that I could do. I wasn't able to show my creative ability to put together my own song because I was given a choice of specifics songs to choose from and I was not allowed to change them. I was only able to give them a little taste of what I'm capable of doing.

There's so much that the world has to offer and there are so many opportunities that have my name on it. With God on my side, the opportunities are endless. I'm anxious to see what the next chapter of my life will bring and to see what the future holds for me.

There's always room for improvement. Up until this very day I am constantly making improvements. Improvement starts with having an open mind. I always critique myself. I look at what I do and see what I could have done better. I never think that I'm too good, or I'm the best. You have to continue to perfect who you are.

I've been booking back to back shows and meeting many different artists from around the world. I have been fortunate enough to make worldwide networking connections that has given me exposure in the way that I didn't have before.

Within the next year, my audience can expect a new album, which we will be shooting a documentary for. We want to show the process and what it takes to make the album. A lot of people don't realize what goes on front to back behind creating music. They don't understand the creative and marketing process and everything that comes after the music is finished. There are many people out here who make great music that don't know what to do after they've made it. When the album is done we're going to put together a bunch of shows. We're going to put together our own headliner shows where we'll have some openers come and perform. We plan on performing in many cities, including my hometown.

In 5 years, I see myself working on my second or third album. Hopefully, I will be at the level that I've been trying to reach for the last 10 years. I want to continue building on the foundation that will be already set and put people in a position to do the same thing in their own way. I will be able to give the people that's closest to me jobs and invest in their dreams and give my family a platform. At the end of the day, it's all about who you know. When I get farther in my career and start making new connections I'll be able to connect people who have similar goals and dreams. Basically, I want to be the gateway to the next level.

Music is like a 10 year thing. When we're known and generating an income, we can make moves and gain power. From the 1st year to the 10th year, it's really just building up as much as we can. Once time and resources start to open up we can make moves and gain power. We will meet different people that will allow me to get into other stuff that's out here in the world. I will start to find other things that I'm interested in…something else that I might fall in love with. But, music is something that I would never get away from. It's the stepping stone to seeing what the rest of the world has to offer. It's a possibility that I may even swing back and start singing again. I've been working on my voice and it's been getting better by finding a range that fits me.

I'm an artistic person. Therefore, in the future, I will start to branch off and dabble in other things. Maybe I'll write a movie or do some acting or something like that. It always comes back to the music. Even if I had a career for 10 years or never put out another album or record I would still find myself in the studio creating music. It's my outlet, it's how I can decompress and get my thoughts in order to continue on. Even when we're not making music we would just sit in the studio. It's been times when we've sat in the studio for like 3 months just talking and watching interviews… studying. That's the kind of love that I have for the music.

"The validation pushes me on. We've been working hits for so long and to have hundreds of thousands of people tell us that we're doing something right makes me ask myself, *how can we touch the world? What's next? It's always what's next, what's after this stage? We can stop here, but what's next, what are we missing? I feel like I can always go higher and higher.*

The chapters never end and the book continues. There are pages of this journey that have not been written yet. There are secrets to success that have not yet been uncovered. The candlestick is still burning and the wax is still dripping down. This is just the beginning for me and I can't wait to see what the future holds. Will you be willing to take this journey with me?

"The mission is never really complete in life period."

For booking information please contact
relljervmusic1@gmail.com

Printed in the United States
By Bookmasters